First World War
and Army of Occupation
War Diary
France, Belgium and Germany

9 DIVISION
3 Lowland Brigades
Cameronians (Scottish Rifles)
8th Battalion.
1 March 1919 - 3 September 1919

WO95/1776/12

The Naval & Military Press Ltd
www.nmarchive.com
Published in association with The National Archives

Published by

The Naval & Military Press Ltd

Unit 10 Ridgewood Industrial Park,

Uckfield, East Sussex,

TN22 5QE England

Tel: +44 (0) 1825 749494

www.naval-military-press.com

www.nmarchive.com

This diary has been reprinted in facsimile from the original. Any imperfections are inevitably reproduced and the quality may fall short of modern type and cartographic standards.

© **Crown Copyright**
Images reproduced by permission of The National Archives, London, England, 2015.

Contents

Document type	Place/Title	Date From	Date To
Heading	Lowland (Late 9th) Division 3 Lowland Bde 1/8 Scottish Rifles 1919 Mar-1919 Sep From 34 Div 103 Bde		
War Diary	Neun Kirchen	01/03/1919	11/03/1919
War Diary	Wahn	12/03/1919	12/03/1919
War Diary	Hilden	13/03/1919	13/03/1919
War Diary	Benrath	14/03/1919	31/03/1919
War Diary	Benrath Germany	01/04/1919	03/04/1919
War Diary	Hilden Germany	04/04/1919	14/05/1919
War Diary	Benrath	15/05/1919	16/05/1919
War Diary	Hilden	17/05/1919	31/05/1919
War Diary	Hilden Germany	01/06/1919	03/06/1919
War Diary	Benrath	03/06/1919	03/06/1919
War Diary	Hilden	04/06/1919	13/06/1919
War Diary	Benrath	14/06/1919	14/06/1919
War Diary	Hilden & Benrath	15/06/1919	15/06/1919
War Diary	Hilden	16/06/1919	30/06/1919
Miscellaneous	Battalion Sports of 8th Batt. The Cameronians (Scottish Rifles)		
Miscellaneous	8th (Cameronians) Scottish Rifles Battalion Sports In Battalion Football Field Walder Strasse Hilden On 29th June 1919	29/06/1919	29/06/1919
Miscellaneous	8th Scottish Rifles Administrative Instructions No. J-3	17/06/1919	17/06/1919
Miscellaneous	1/8 Bn. Scottish Rifles Orders for Relief of Coys. on Outpost	19/06/1919	19/06/1919
Operation(al) Order(s)	1/8th Scottish Rifles Operation Order No.2	23/06/1919	23/06/1919
Operation(al) Order(s)	1/8th Scottish Rifles Operation Order No.3	29/06/1919	29/06/1919
War Diary	Hilden Germany	01/07/1919	07/07/1919
War Diary	Konigshoven	08/07/1919	14/07/1919
War Diary	Konigshoven Germany	14/07/1919	31/07/1919
Miscellaneous	Inter-Allied Sports Meeting		
Miscellaneous	Results		
Miscellaneous	Weekly Training Programme		
War Diary	Konigshoven	01/08/1919	31/08/1919
Operation(al) Order(s)	1/8th Scottish Rifles Operation Order No.4	06/08/1919	06/08/1919
Miscellaneous	Transfer Of The Battalion To The U.K General Administrative Instructions No.5 To Accompany Operation Order No.5		
War Diary	Germany Konigshoven	01/09/1919	01/09/1919
War Diary	France	02/09/1919	03/09/1919

LOWLAND (LATE 9th) DIVISION

3 LOWLAND BDE

1/8 SCOTTISH RIFLES

1919 MAR — 1919 SEP

From 34 DIV, 103 BDE

War From 3D to 103rd Div.

1/6 Scottish Rifles

Vol 12

WAR DIARY or **INTELLIGENCE SUMMARY**
Army Form C. 2118.
(Erase heading not required.)

Instructions regarding War Diaries and Intelligence Summaries are contained in F.S. Regs. Part II and the Staff Manual respectively. Title pages will be prepared in manuscript.

Place	Date	Hour	Summary of Events and Information	Remarks and references to Appendices
NEUNKIRCHEN	1919 MARCH 11 to MARCH 11		Holding the outpost line at Neunkirchen - nothing of importance to note. Men in very comfortable billets. Very little training was possible, owing to very scattered areas occupied by the Battalion. The ability of Educational classes were however maintained	
WAHN	" 12		Relieved by the 6th A.Bn. Royal West Kent Regt. whose relief commenced at 6-30. Battalion marched to HENNEF & entrained 15-15. Detrained at WAHN at 16-00, marched to Barracks & came under the command of 101st Bde. Bde. Bde. Bn. Staff 10 Officers & 76 ORs from 18th 9th Scottish Rifles reported to us for duty.	
HILDEN	" 13		Bn. Hd.Qrs at 09.00 & entrained for HILDEN arriving at HILDEN at 10-30 & came under the command of 28th Bde 9th Div. Marched to billets at Benrath. Experienced some difficulty in settling down, owing to the distance between billets.	
BENRATH	" 14		Spent the day in settling down, men fairly comfortable. Draft of 15 Officers & 158 ORs from 2nd HLI reported for duty, posted to Companies.	
"	" 15			
"	" 16 to 19		Companies organising & training.	

Army Form C. 2118.

WAR DIARY
or
INTELLIGENCE SUMMARY.
(Erase heading not required.)

Place	Date	Hour	Summary of Events and Information	Remarks and references to Appendices
BENRATH	MARCH 20		Battalion detailed to serve night Sub sector of Bde. outpost-line working parties of 10 Officers & 140 O.R.s daily. Remainder of Btn. training under Company Comdrs.	
"	21 to 31		Wiring daily, strength of parties increased. "Z" Coy took over Guard duties at RHENANIA PETROLEUM Works on 27th & struck off all working parties. Arrangements completed for move of Btn. to HILDEN to relieve 1st London Scottish at some near future date.	

J. Edward
Major
Comdg. 18th Durham Rifles

Army Form C. 2118.

WAR DIARY
or
INTELLIGENCE SUMMARY.
(Erase heading not required)

1/8th. Scottish Rifles.

Instructions regarding War Diaries and Intelligence Summaries are contained in F.S. Regs., Part II. and the Staff Manual respectively. Title pages will be prepared in manuscript.

Place	Date	Hour	Summary of Events and Information	Remarks and references to Appendices
BENRATH, GERMANY.	April, 1st. 2nd.		Major Eaves, D.S.O. is still Commanding the Battalion. Two Companies, "W" and "Y" training, section training chiefly, as laid down in the programme issued by Divisional H.Q. "Z" Coy. are still on duty at the Rhenania Petrol Works. "X" Coy. are finding all the duties and providing wiring parties for the R.E's.	
	3rd.		Battalion moved by road to HILDEN, 2½ miles from BENRATH and took over billets vacated by the 1st. London Scottish. Men are very comfortable and there are beds for all, messing arrangements are very good.	
HILDEN, GERMANY.	4th. 5th. 6th. 7th. to 30th.		Spent the two days in settling down in new billets. The civil population are civil and quiet. there seems to be no unrest here. Church Parades. "W" and "Y" Coys. training each week. Hours of work 09.30 to 12.30. Lewis Gun and Signalling Classes are also held, with recreational training, football etc. in the afternoons. "X" Coy. finding all the wiring parties and guards. General Girdwood, C.B. inspected the Guard found by us for Divisional Hqrs. and expressed his satisfaction on the 9th. Lt. Col. Clark returned from leave on the 8th. and resumed Command. Major Eaves taking over the duties of 2nd. in Command. Nothing of any importance to report until the 13th. when Lt. Col., Findlay, D.S.O. arrived to take over the Command of the Battalion from Lt. Col. Clark. The demobilization is progressing very well and we have now only 2 Officers and 59 men still to demobilize. Leave too, is quite plentiful. We have had a good issue of clothing and boots, each man is now in possession of two suits. The Battalion is now comfortably settled down in HILDEN, and everything working smoothly. The Battalion Workshops are all running well and turning out a lot of work. The numbers with the Battalion Football Team played the 11th. Royal Scots on the 30th, and was defeated by one goal to nothing, after a good game. The numbers with the Battalion on the 30th. are Officers 26 Other Ranks, 538.	

Lt. Col.,
Cmdg. 1/8th. Scottish Rifles.

Army Form C. 2118.

WAR DIARY
or
INTELLIGENCE SUMMARY.
(Erase heading not required.)

Instructions regarding War Diaries and Intelligence Summaries are contained in F. S. Regs., Part II. and the Staff Manual respectively. Title pages will be prepared in manuscript.

Place	Date	Hour	Summary of Events and Information	Remarks and references to Appendices
HILDEN GERMANY	May 1st.		Effective Strength of Battalion: Officers 38, O.Rs. 697. Ration strength 26 Officers, 538 O.Rs. "X" and "Y" Coys. are still training; "W" Coy. are finding all the duties; "Z" Coy. are on duty at RHENANIA Petrol Works. "W", "X", and "Y" Companies wired on the Battalion front to-day under the R.Es. 500 yards of double apron put out. Cinema performance in The Hilden Theatre at 17.30.	
do.	2nd.		"X" and "Y" Coys. training. "X" Coy. on the Range at Urdenbach firing. The Lewis Gunners under instruction also fired to-day.	
do.	3rd.		Lt. Col. Findlay, D.S.O. left the Battalion to assume temporary command of the 3rd. Lowland Inf. Bde. in the absence of Brig. Gen. Girdwood, C.B. Major Eaves, D.S.O. assumed temporary command of the Battalion. "X", "Y" and "W" Coys. spent the morning in interior economy. Half day's holiday.	
do.	4th.		Church Parades. The Officers of the Battalion played the Officers of the 9th. Scottish Rifles at football, and won 1-0.	
do.	5th.		"X" and "Y" Coys. training; men of "W" Coy. not employed on guards, wiring. We sent 4 officers and 8 N.C.Os. to a general course held at Hilden by Lt. Morris, II Corps Hqrs., for 1 week. Cinema Show at 17.30.	
do.	6th.		"X" Company on the range at Urdenbach firing. "Y" Coy. platoon training, "W" Coy. wiring.	
do.	7th.		"W", "X", and "Y" Companies all wiring from 09.15 to 12.30. Baths for "W" and "X" Coys. in the afternoon.	
do.	8th.		"X" and "Y" Coys. training on Battn. Football field, "W" Coy. wiring.	
do.	9th.		"Y" Company on the Range, "X" Coy. training, "W" Coy. wiring. A lecture was given by Mr. J. J. McCabe on "Life in the Past Ages" at 15.30 in the Realschule, Hilden.	

Army Form C. 2118.

WAR DIARY
or
INTELLIGENCE SUMMARY.
(Erase heading not required.)

Instructions regarding War Diaries and Intelligence Summaries are contained in F.S. Regs., Part II. and the Staff Manual respectively. Title pages will be prepared in manuscript.

Place	Date	Hour	Summary of Events and Information	Remarks and references to Appendices
HILDEN GERMANY	May 10th.		"W", "X", and "Y" Coys. Interior Economy and cleaning up. Half Day's holiday. The Battalion football team played the 11th. Royal Scots, on our own ground, result 1-1. Some trouble has arisen between the civilian Employers and Employees, with the result that the latter have come out on strike. We are ordered to send 2 platoons to proceed as guard over the RHENISCH Power Station, HOLTHAUSEN. "W" Coy. provided these platoons, who are in position by 16.00	
do.	11th.		Church Parades and holiday. "W" Company sent 1 platoon from Hilden to reinforce "Z" Coy. at Himmelgeist Control Post; move complete at 12.30 hours. The strike still continues. "X" Coy. takes over from "W" Company all guards, duties, etc. as from to-day, owing to "W" Coy. being reduced to 2 platoons.	
do.	12th.		The Remainder of "Y" Company (3 platoons and Hqrs.) moved to Himmelgeist and relieved detachment of "Z" Company there. "Y" Coy. are now all at Himmelgeist. Remaining 2 platoons of "W" Company in Hilden proceeded to Rhenania and took over from two platoons of "Z" Coy. All of "Z" Company returned to Hilden and took over billets vacated by "W" Company. All reliefs complete by 15.00 hours. The two platoons of "W" Coy. at the Power Station joined their Coy. at Rhenania. "X" Company are now finding all duties.	
do.	13th.		Only 2 Companies now in Hilden. No training to-day. "Z" Coy. are settling down in new billets and "X" Company fully employed on guards, etc.	
do.	14th.		Owing to the Civil disturbances (strikes) "Z", "X", and Battn. Hqrs. moved to Benrath to-day. Hqrs. and "Z" Coy. billeted in the Schloss Hotel, and "X" Company at Rhenania. Move was complete by 18.00 hours.	
BENRATH.	15th.		"X" and "Z" Coys. remained in Benrath and marched round Factories in the morning to ensure that the strikers were at work. Everything quiet, and strike seems to have been settled.	
do.	16th.		Hqrs., "X", and "Z" Coys. moved back to Hilden: arrived at 10.00 hours. All attended a lecture at 10.30 in the Realschule, Hilden, By Brig. Gen. Stone.	
HILDEN.	17th.		"X" and "Z" Companies, Interior Economy; half day's holiday. "W" Coy. are now all at Rhenania, and "Y" all at Himmelgeist, having just sufficient men to carry out all their Coy. duties.	

Army Form C. 2118.

WAR DIARY
of
INTELLIGENCE SUMMARY.

(Erase heading not required.)

Instructions regarding War Diaries and Intelligence Summaries are contained in F.S. Regs., Part II. and the Staff Manual respectively. Title pages will be prepared in manuscript.

Place	Date	Hour	Summary of Events and Information	Remarks and references to Appendices
HILDEN.	18th.		Church Parades and Holiday. Lt. Col. Findlay, D.S.O. returned from Bde. and resumed command of the Battalion.	
do.	19th.		"Z" Company training; "X" Coy. took over from the 9th. Sco. Rifles the Holthausen Barrier and Control Post. Garrison: 3 Officers, 8 N.C.Os., 30 O.Rs. This leaves practically only one Company, with Battn. Hqrs., in Hilden. Relief was complete by 16.00 hours. Our detachment of 1 Off. and 12 O.Rs. of "Y" Coy. from Friedhof Post rejoined their Company to-day at Himmelgeist. "Z" Coy. took over all duties to-day from "X" Coy.	
do.	20th.		Practically no training except specialists can be carried out now, only one Company ("Z") being available, and they have to find all duties in the Battalion. A party from the Battn. of 2 Officers and 15 O.Rs. proceeded on a steamer trip up the Rhine to-day, leaving Hilden at 07.30 hours and returning at 23.45 hours.	
do.	21st.		Nothing of note to report. All men in the Battalion are fully employed, and we have great difficulty in finding any men for training, even specialists. Divn. Hdqrs. Guard found by us to-day of 1 Sergt., 2 Corpls., and 18 Privates, who go on duty for 1 week.	
do.	22nd.		No training. All men fully employed on guards, etc. Nothing of note to report.	
do.	23rd.		All available men of "Z" and Hqrs. Details attended a Lecture "In Shakespearian Atmosphere" by Mr. Kirwan in the Realschule, Hilden. Nothing else of note to report.	
do.	24th.		Interior Economy and cleaning up for Hdqrs. Details and "Z" Coy. Half day's holiday.	
do.	25th.		Church Parades and Holiday.	
do.	26th.		All men employed. No training.	
do.	27th.		No training. Inspection of billets, messes, and Regt. Institutes by the Divisional Cmdr., Major Gen. Butler, C.M.G., who afterwards spoke to all available officers in the Hdqrs. Mess.	

Army Form C. 2118.

WAR DIARY
or
INTELLIGENCE SUMMARY.
(Erase heading not required.)

Instructions regarding War Diaries and Intelligence Summaries are contained in F.S. Regs., Part II. and the Staff Manual respectively. Title pages will be prepared in manuscript.

Place	Date	Hour	Summary of Events and Information	Remarks and references to Appendices
HILDEN.	27th.	(ctd.)	Lecture for Coy. Officers at 11.00 by a Sergt. of the II Corps on the "Use of Carrier Pigeons". Lt. Gen. Jacobs, II Corps Cmdr., called at Hdqrs. at 12.30 hours.	
do.	28th.		Divisional Guard returns to Battalion. Another Civilian strike breaks out in Hilden and Benrath; we send a guard of 1 Officer and 15 O.Rs. from "Z" Coy. to the Hilden waterworks to safeguard the workmen remaining on duty and prevent any interference with the works themselves. A proclamation is issued forbidding circulation of civilians except between the hours of 06.00 and 18.00. All Cafes are closed; no meetings to be held; no lights allowed (civilian) after 22.00; and no groups of more than 5 people allowed to congregate in the streets. The civilian population appear to accept the situation quietly.	
do.	29th.		Ascension Day. The Germans are still on strike, but very quiet. A number of strike leaders arrested by us and removed to Benrath. No training.	
do.	30th.		The strike continues; more arrests are made and the leaders put over the perimeter into the Unoccupied Territory. No training.	
do.	31st.		The Strikers return to work; a few still remain away. No training. We have demobilized during the month of May; Officers 2, O.Rs. 65.	
			Effective Strength of Battalion to-day 30 Officers, 626 O.Rs, " " " " 19 " 443 " Ration	

Army Form C. 2118.

WAR DIARY
or
~~INTELLIGENCE SUMMARY.~~
(Erase heading not required.)

1/8th. Bn. SCOTTISH RIFLES.

Place	Date	Hour	Summary of Events and Information	Remarks and references to Appendices
HILDEN GERMANY.	June 1st.		There have been the usual Church Parades, and the day has been observed locally as a public holiday by the German inhabitants. The Strike has now ended, and the proclamation issued on the 28th. ult. has been amended to read: "Cafes are open from 10.00 – 18.00 hours, and circulation is allowed till 20.00 hours."	
	2nd.		All men are employed, and no training is possible. There is nothing of note to report. Education classes are now ordered to be held 3 times a week, viz. Monday, Wednesday, and Friday.	
	3rd.		This was the King's Birthday, and was accordingly celebrated as a general holiday among the local troops. The Bn. paraded along with the 1/4th. R.S.F. and a Detachment of the Tank Corps. (who are stationed in HILDEN in view of any developments of a military nature) on the Parade Ground of the Fusiliers, Lt. Colonel Findlay, D.S.O., O.C. Troops, HILDEN, being in charge of the massed parade. The Parade saluted the Flag, and three lusty cheers were given for the King before marching off. At the Schloss, BENRATH, were Sports and Amusements of every sort, catering for all tastes; and among the equestrian events the Battn. carried off 2 of the mile races. There was much hilarity throughout the Meeting.	
BENRATH.				
HILDEN.	4th.		The day was uneventful, and there was no training.	
	5th. 6th. 7th. 8th.		There is nothing of note to report.	
			The usual Church Parades were held only.	
	9th.		By order of the O.-in-C., the day – being Whit Monday – was observed as a holiday; there was no training done, and the Workshops were closed all day.	
	10th.		There being no training, one officer and ten O.R. proceeded on the Rhine Steamer Trip, leaving HILDEN at 07.00 hours and returning at 23.00 hours.	
	11th. 12th. 13th.		No training was done, as all men were still employed during the day.	
BENRATH.	14th.		Being a half-holiday, the day was a busy one at the Schloss, where a Garden Fete had been organized by the Bde. Amusements Officer (Capt. Stavers, R.S.F.) in the ground around the Schloss itself. The Battn. had its own Marquee erected, and there the Officers had tea and dinner, entertaining numerous guests, among whom were several ladies of the Miss Lena	

Army Form C. 2118.

WAR DIARY

(Erase heading not required.)

1/8th. BN. SCOTTISH RIFLES.

Instructions regarding War Diaries and Intelligence Summaries are contained in F. S. Regs., Part II. and the Staff Manual respectively. Title pages will be prepared in manuscript.

Place	Date	Hour	Summary of Events and Information	Remarks and references to Appendices
	JUNE			
BENRATH	14th.		Ashwell Concert Party, and some Staff Officers from neighbouring formations. The Programme included Mule Races, tug-o'-war and foot races. Two bands were present, viz. that of the 17th. Lancers and the American Jazz Band, who greatly delighted the large crowd present at the Fête. At 19.00 hours, in the open air, an excellent concert was given by Lena Ashwell's Concert Party, the programme including songs, humorous and sentimental. The men of the Battn. who were present were served with tea in the ground, and thoroughly enjoyed the day.	
HILDEN & BENRATH.	15th.		Church Parades were held, and in the afternoon the Fête went merrily on, both bands being still present, and at 19.00 hours an impromptu concert was held in the open. So passed another day of enjoyment for the troops.	
HILDEN.	16th.		There was no military training, but 15 men have attended the voluntary educational classes under 2/Lt. Telfer, Bn. Ed. O., who has arranged that classes will meet thrice weekly. Coys. have just sufficient men to find the various duties called for.	
	17th.		There has been training again, but we have begun to prepare for a Move. We are to go forward owing to the enemy having further delayed the signing of the Peace. In the event of the Hun not having signed by a certain stipulated time. All surplus baggage has been stacked at the Bde. Dump in the Realschule, HILDEN, and is being guarded by a party of 6 men under 2/Lt. Patterson, of "Z" Coy. Transport arrangements have been made to enable the 3 outlying Coys. to move as soon as required. The 6th. Royal Highlanders (Black Watch) have sent an Advance Party to reconnoitre billets, and to ascertain the duties which their Battn. will take over from us. The relieving Battn. is expected to arrive to-morrow. The Billeting arrangements for the B. Watch have all been done by the Rifles to facilitate their settling comfortably as quickly as possible.	
	18th.		In consequence of further orders, preparations are still in progress for the Move; to-morrow will be "the day", and everybody is keen. At 18.00 hours the R. Highlanders arrived at HILDEN STN., where our cookers met them, supplying boiling water for their tea after the train journey. All surplus stores have been properly disposed of, and orders issued for the concentration of all Coy. at HILDEN. We almost hope for a Move. Arrangements have been made for tram cars to bring down with Coy. Stores. "W", and "X" Coys., who are at Rhenania Petrol Installation, HOLTHAUSEN, and HIMMELGEIST respectively. We are to concentrate at HILDEN.	
	19th.		The Move has been postponed, owing to an extension of time to the Bosche for the signing of the Peace Terms. About 18.00 hours "W", "X", and "Y" Coys. arrived by tram, having been relieved by the 8th. Black Watch. By 19.30 hours the 3 Coys. are settled in billets, and all seem pleased to be back with H.Q. at HILDEN, after the quiet tedium of the Petrol Factory, the bustle of HOLTHAUSEN Barrier, and the nightly patrols at HIMMELGEIST. It seems good to be	

Army Form C. 2118.

3.

WAR DIARY
or
~~INTELLIGENCE SUMMARY~~
(Erase heading not required.)

1/8th. BN. SCOTTISH RIFLES.

Instructions regarding War Diaries and Intelligence Summaries are contained in F. S. Regs., Part II. and the Staff Manual respectively. Title pages will be prepared in manuscript.

Place	Date	Hour	Summary of Events and Information	Remarks and references to Appendices
HILDEN.	JUNE 19th.		home again! Now we are ready to move at one hour's notice. Lt. Burke, D.S.O., with his Section of M.G.C. arrived, and will be attached to the Battalion during the operations, which seem imminent.	
	20th.		Coys. spent the day settling in billets and in doing any final packing required.	
	21st.		The Bn. being together again, the Cmdg. Officer had a Battalion parade. Coys. were inspected in Fighting Order by the Battn. Comdr., and then we did some ceremonial drill. Considering how recently we have just moved, leaving our "best suits" in the Surplus Baggage Dump, the "turn out" of the men is good, but the drill is slack, for tracking smugglers and patrolling at nights have not helped our drill. We will do better next time, however.	
	22nd.		Church Parades were held as usual, and we receive orders that Zero hour is 03.15 hours to-morrow. Then we will start our advance into Hun Unoccupied Territory. The War will begin again.	
	23rd.		The Move is suspended at 01.30 hours! We will not move yet. The day is spent in cleaning up.	
	24th.		Now we are back to the square again, and the Coys. are at the disposal of their Commanders for training.	
	25th.		The Colonel has another Bn. Parade, and inspects the Bn. in Battle Order. This time we have improved in turn-out, and in drill we have done some ceremonial that none of us has done for many a day. We are finding ourselves again. We worked from 10.00 - 12.30 hours.	
	26th.		The Bn. Football Field was the starting point for our Route March. We paraded as strong as possible, and formed up in Mass. We marched via HULSEN, PAULSMÜHLE, and returned along the main BENRATH-HILDEN Road; en route we met the Brigade Cmdr., who informed C.O. that Coys. would likely be required to relieve Coys. of the Black Watch in the Outpost Line, if Peace were signed. During 2 stretches of road exercises in Visual Training were practised; in the first instance men were required to make a note of all manner of food stuffs passed on the way which would prove useful to troops advancing; men noted cattle, goats, poultry, and crops, and some even made out a brief statement showing how many they thought could be rationed out of their larder. Prizes were offered by the Cmdg. Officer for the best "Observation Report" submitted by each Coy. Later in the march men numbered the broken windows they passed on a given stretch of road. The marching throughout was good. Orders for the withdrawal of surplus baggage from the Realschule Dump were issued to-day. Lt. Calder took over command of "X" Coy. vice Capt. Dalrymple, M.C., who proceeded on leave to-day, while Capt. E. R. Saltonstall, M.O. reported to 3rd. Lowland Bde. to officiate as	

Army Form C. 2118.

4.

WAR DIARY

or

~~INTELLIGENCE SUMMARY~~

1/8th. BN. SCOTTISH RIFLES.

(*Erase heading not required.*)

Instructions regarding War Diaries and Intelligence Summaries are contained in F. S. Regs., Part II. and the Staff Manual respectively. Title pages will be prepared in manuscript.

Place	Date	Hour	Summary of Events and Information	Remarks and references to Appendices
HILDEN.	JUNE 26th.		Staff Captain, the duties of Adjutant being taken over by Capt. George Menary, M.C., who vacated command of "W" Coy. Lieut. F.S.V. Barr, M.C. assumed command of "W" Coy.	
	27th.		The weather being wet, training was carried on in billets, and men rilled in the last hour of the morning clearing up for the Bn. Panoramic Photograph, to be taken in the afternoon by the Official Photographer from G.H.Q.; "W" and "X", H.Q. and Transport, "Y" and "Z" Coys. were taken together, then followed a group of the Officers, and of the W.Os. and Sergeants. A brave show! The Cmdg. Officer and Adjutant looked in to see the members of the Sergeants' Mess before dinner, and for an informal talk. It was suggested to-night that we endeavour to have Bn. Sports while the Bn. was yet concentrated; in case we might disperse again on Monday first. Sunday, 29th. inst. was suggested as the most suitable day.	
	28th.		Coys. are at the disposal of Coy. Cmdrs. to-day for Interior Economy. O.C. visited Transport and the M.O. inspected "Y" and "Z" Coys. The Sports Committee issued their Programme of Events this morning before breakfast, and if only the weather is good, we should have a splendid gathering. The C.O. and Adjutant called at the Sergts.' Mess at 13.30 hours, and the Colonel made a few apposite remarks on the importance of the Non-Commissioned Officer in the maintenance of discipline, and in the cultivation of esprit de corps in a battalion. Again at 9 p.m. the Bn. Cmdr., Major Eaves, D.S.O., Capt. Nicholl, Lt. Young and the Adjutant visited the Sergts.' Mess for the presentation of the Whist Drive prizes by the Colonel. The tone of the Mess was good and well 'run' by its President. The Sports Secy. and his Committee are working hard.	
	29th.		During the forenoon a party from each Coy. was engaged on preparing the football pitch for our Sports in the afternoon; Church Parades were consequently weak. At 14.00 hours the Sports began and continued till 18.30 hours, when the prizes were presented by Brigadier-General Girdwood, C.B., C.M.G., Cmdg. 3rd. Lowland Bde. A programme and account of the whole proceedings are appended. After Supper the Officers attended the concert in "W" Coy's. Billet, the old gym, where an extremely good programme was rendered, the artistes being both officers and men. We finished off at 22.45 hours.	
	30th.		The morning was devoted to packing all stores for the move this afternoon. At 14.00 hours "W", "X", and "Z" Coys. boarded trams for HIMMELGEIST, HOLTHAUSEN, and RHENANIA Petrol Factory at HOLTHAUSEN, to relieve Coys. of 8th. B.W. "Relief complete" was reported by 17.00 hours. Now only "Y" Coy. and Bn. H.Q. are left at HILDEN.	

Army Form C. 2118.

WAR DIARY

~~INTELLIGENCE SUMMARY~~

(Erase heading not required.)

1/8th. BN. SCOTTISH RIFLES.

Instructions regarding War Diaries and Intelligence Summaries are contained in F. S. Regs., Part II. and the Staff Manual respectively. Title pages will be prepared in manuscript.

Place	Date	Hour	Summary of Events and Information	Remarks and references to Appendices
HILDEN	JUNE 30th.		We have demobilized during the month............4	
			Effective Strength of Battn. to-day, 30 Officers, 651 O.Rs.	
			" " " " 22 " 530 " Ration	
			George Murray	
			(Lt-x-4a5) Lt. Col.,	
			Comdg. 1/8th. Scottish Rifles,	
			British Army of the Rhine.	

BATTALION SPORTS
of
8th. Batt. The Cameronians (Scottish Rifles).

The Sports of the 8th. Batt. The Cameronians (Scottish Rifles) took place at Hilden on Sunday, 29th. June, before a large concourse of spectators.

The tastily printed programmes shewed a galaxy of events, there being no fewer than twenty-one.

The flat races attracted large entries and the two open events, the mile and the 440 yards, drew good fields and furnished some excellent running.

A feature of the short distance races was the attractive sprinting of Capt. E.R. Saltonstall, late Adjt., of the battalion, who produced splendid form, worthy of one who had run at Olympic Games.

The miscellaneous races were a source of much amusement, the boat race, three-legged and palliasse races especially, appealing to the large German spectatorate round the ropes.

Much credit redounded on the Transport section of the unit for the great show they made, both in the number of events they provided and in the excellence of their efforts. In the Alarm Race one did not know what to admire the more, the dexterity of the drivers in harnessing the animals or the fleetness of the horses when they got off their mark.

The mounted men also did well in the keenly contested Tug-of-War, as after an intense struggle they vanquished "Z" Coy., who had already laid low a team of which much was expected.

Much hilarity and merriment was caused by the appearance on the field of certain 'ladies', garbed in what certainly could be called 'the latest fashion'. Several disported themselves on mule back in such a way as would have caused the 'unco guid' to have raised their hands to heaven in pious horror, but which elicited shrieks of laughter from the assembled crowd.

At intervals during the afternoon the pipers of the 11th. Royal Scots played selections and the wild skirling of the pipes obviously awed the Huns, who to all appearances were less interested in a local Instrumental Band which also played tasteful airs.

Tea and refreshments were served on the ground and at the conclusion of the Sports the prizes were presented by Brig. General E.S. Girdwood, C.B., C.M.G., 3rd. Lowland Inf. Bde., who afterwards on the motion of Lt. Col. Findlay, D.S.O., comdg. the 8th. Cameronians, was heartily cheered. Among other spectators were Lt. Col. Mc.Kenzie, 3rd. Lowland Division, Lt. Col. Green, 6th. Royal Highlanders, and numerous Officers and men from both Lowland and Highland Divisions.

A proposed Camp Fire Concert had to be abandoned owing to a heavy shower of rain, but this was no loss, for a great audience gathered in the well equipped Recreation Hall of the Battalion and listened with rapt attention to a splendid recital of song and story. C.S.M. Searles as a comedian made a great hit, and the singing of Pte. Ward was much appreciated, while Pte. Thomson in the 'Yukon Trail' impressed everyone by a wonderful dramatic display. After a speech by the Colonel the proceedings terminated with the singing of the National Anthem and Auld Lang Syne.

Much of the success of the Sports was due to the splendid organisation of the Sports Committee and to the energetic fashion in which they did their work.

Result of the Events.

Mules Scurry. 1. Wilson, 2. Aitken, 3. Agnew.
100 yards. 1. Nicol, 2. Mc.Kelvie, 3. Lowie.
Wheelbarrow Race. 1. Kay & Anderson, 2. Mc.Millan & Ramsay, 3. Whitehill & Campbell.
1 Mile (open) 1. Thirwall (R.E.), 2. Grabham, (M.G.C.), 3. Plummer, (M.G.C.)
Best Turn Out. 1. Clark, 2. & 3. divided Marshall & Smith.
Boat Race. "Y" Coy.
Tug-of-War. 1. Transport, 2. "Z" Coy.
V.C. Race. 1. Ross, 2. Renwick, 3. Aitken.
Three legged Race. 1. Anderson, & Kay, 2. Thomson & Neville.
100 yards Old Soldier's Race. 1. Matthews, 2. Searles, 3. Ryan.
440 yards (Open). 1. Plummer (M.G.C.), 2. Salvona, 3. Cassels.
Slow Cycle Race. 1. Taylor.

Best Comic Turn Out. 1. (divided) Searles & Coffield, 2. Carmichael.
Wrestling on mules. 1. Cruikshanks, 2. Wilson.
220 yards. 1. Warburton, 2. Salvona, 3. Badger.
'Wooden Spoon' (Officer's mule race) Capt. Brook.
Palliasse Race. 1. Darlison, 2. Anderson.
Alarm Race. 1. Ross, 2. Agnew, 3. Devaney.
Driving Competition. 1. Gibson.
Singing Competition. 1. Thomson, 2. Ward.
Best Company Aggregate. 'Y' Coy.
Totak Prize Money Value of 3000 marks.

8th. (Cameronians) Scottish Rifles

Battalion Sports

in

Battalion Football Field, Walder Strasse
HILDEN

on 29th June 1919 commencing at 14.00 hours.

Programme of Events.

1. Mules Scurry for N. C. O's. and men
   Prizes 50 : 25 : 10 marks
2. 100 yds. Race
   Prizes 100 : 50 : 30 marks
3. Wheelbarrow Race
   Prizes 60 : 30 : 10 marks
4. 1 Mile Scratch Race (Open to Brigade)
   Prizes 200 : 100 : 50 marks
5. Best Turn out of pair of Horses or Mules, with Harness
   Prizes 100 : 50 : 25 marks
6. Boat Race (Coy. Teams of 8.)
   Prizes for winners 80 marks
7. Tug of War (Coy. Teams of 10.)
   Prizes 300 : 200 marks
8. Relay Race of 100, 220, 440, 220 yds. (Coy. Teams, comprising Coy. Commander, C. S. M. C. Q. M. S and 1 Pte.)
   Prizes 90 : 40 marks
9. V. C. Race (Horses)
   Prizes 50 : 30 : 10 marks
10. Three-legged Race
    Prizes 40 : 20 marks
11. 150 yds. Old Soldiers' Race (1 yd. start for every year's service over 5 years.)
    Prizes 50 : 20 : 10 marks
12. 440 yds. Race. (Open to Brigade)
    Prizes 100 : 50 : 25 marks
13. Slow Cycle Race.
    Prize 25 marks
14. Best Comic Turn Out. (Fancy Dress)
    Prizes 100 : 50 marks
15. Wrestling on Mules.
    Prizes 100 : 50 marks
16. 220 yds. Race.
    Prizes 60 : 30 : 20 marks
17. Hilden "Wooden Spoon" for Officers — Mule Race — (Officers not riding forfeit 5 marks ea. proceeds to go to the winner.)
18. Paliasse Race
    Prizes 50 : 25 marks
19. Alarm Race (Horses)
    Prizes 75 : 50 : 25 marks
20. Driving Competition.
    Prize 100 marks
21. Jumping Competition for Officers, N. C. O's and men (Mounted).

A Band will be in attendance

Tea will be served on the field during the afternoon.

Free refreshments will be given in the course of the proceedings in exchange for the vouchers issued by Companies.

Grande Finale

After the conclusion of the Sports

a

Camp-Fire Smoking Concert

will be held at which additional Prizes will be given for the Best Turns.

The Sports Prizes will be presented
by
Brig. General E. S. Girdwood, C. B., C. M. G.
Commanding, 3rd Lowland Inf. Bde.

9TH. SCOTTISH RIFLES.   Appendix I
                                          17/6/19
ADMINISTRATIVE INSTRUCTIONS. No. J - 3 (to-day).

1. **DISPOSAL OF SURPLUS KITS.**

   (a). All surplus baggage, including one blanket per man, second suit, crockery, mess property, recreational kit, educational books; surplus rifles, box respirators, steel helmets of people on leave, which cannot be carried on the available transport, will be stored at the REALSCHULE by J + 1 day in the accomodation which has been allotted to this unit. Each Coy. will send a storeman with the surplus baggage to look after it.

   J-1

   (b). All surplus officers' kits will also be sent in, the maximum weight per officer which is permitted in first line transport being 35 lbs.

   (c). 2/Lt. D. M. Patterson, 1 N.C.O. from "Z" Coy., 1 storeman from each Coy., 1 representative from Q.M. Stores, and 1 representative from Officers Mess will remain at the REALSCHULE in charge of the Battalion's stores. The Q.M. will leave 3 days complete rations for this personnel.

2. **DISPOSAL OF AREA AND REQUISITIONED STORES.**

   (a). **PALIASSES.** Coys. will make their own arrangements with regard to the emptying of paliasses. The empty cases will then be sent to REALSCHULE" HILDEN.

   (b). **CUTLERY.** "X" and "Y" Coys. will hand over their cutlery to the relieving unit, obtaining receipts from them in triplicate.

3. **NUCLEUS.** There will be no nucleus of the Battalion left behind.

4. **RELIEF.** The 6th. Royal Highlanders will relieve this unit on the afternoon of J - 2 day, billets being arranged between the Adjutant and their advance party. All billeting returns will be completed and forwarded to the Staff Captain, Civil Duties, on vacation of billets.

5. **TRANSPORT.**

   (a). **LORRIES.** 2 lorries are allotted to the Battalion for the transport of packs and one blanket per man (to be rolled in bundles of 10) and the necessary stores in their order of priority. These lorries will report at H.Q. at 16.00 hours on J - @ day, and will be sent back to KRONPRINZ Factory, OHLIGS, after the first day's march.
   Coys. will stack their packs and blankets in the square outside the Church, HILDEN, ready for loading at a time to be notified later.

   (b). **AMMUNITION, GRENADES, and VEREY LIGHTS.** First line transport will carry the full establishment of S.A.A. and Verey Lights. Outpost Coys. will send back to Q.M. Stores their surplus Verey Lights and S.A.A.

   (c). **LEWIS GUNS.** Lewis Guns will be sent down on J - 2 day with the surplus baggage, with the exception of one gun each with the Coys. at HIMMELGEIST and HOLTHAUSEN.

   (d). **WATER.** Water carts and Water Bottles will move full.

6. **STABLING.**

   (a). No stabling will be taken over until it is disinfected. Until this is done all animals will be picketed in the open.

   (b). No wooden troughs or wooden racks will be used until after they have been disinfected.

   (c). Animals to be watered in the lines, water buckets being

(2).

being used until troughs are available.

(d). No civilian forges are to be used. Horses are to be shod in their own lines.

7. PERSONNEL & RECEPTION CAMP.

Personnel returning from leave on J - 1 day and subsequent days will be met by 2/Lt. D. M. Patterson at Personnel ~~Reloading Point~~ Railhead, OHLIGS, under arrangements made by the Commandant, Divisional Reception Camp. They will be conducted to the REALSCHULE, HILDEN, where eachman will be issued with his rifle, 120 rounds S.A.A., Box Respirator and steel helmet.

8. CLOTHING.

Surplus stocks of clean underclothing will be stored in the REALSCHULE, HILDEN. Coys. will send these with their surplus stores. Dirty underclothing to be returned to Bde. Stores will be sent in with the surplus kits to-morrow, earmarked for the Q.M. Stores, in order that it may be sent in from there.

17/6/19.

Capt. & Adjt.,
1/8 Scottish Rifles.

COPY NO. 10

SECRET.   1/8 Bn. SCOTTISH RIFLES.   COPY NO. 10

Appendix VI

ORDERS FOR RELIEF OF COYS. ON OUTPOST.

REF. MAP DUSSELDORF, sheet 4, 1/25,000.   10th. June, 1919.

1. The Perimeter Posts and Guards now held by the 3rd. Lowland Brigade will be relieved to-day (10th. June) by the 3rd. Highland Brigade.

2. The 3 Companies of this Battalion on duty respectively at HOLTHAUSEN, HIMMELGEIST, and RHENANIA Petrol Factory, will be relieved by detachments of the 8th. Black Watch at approximately 15.00 hours.

   (2a). Trams to convey the Coys. to HILDEN will be at the following places, at these times:—

   Tram for Coy. from HOLTHAUSEN BARRIER;   HOLTHAUSEN JUNCT. 16.00
   "   "   "   " HIMMELGEIST: "   "   17.00
   "   "   "   " RHENANIA Petrol Factory, BENRATH "   16.30

   Coys. will detram in the Square facing the Y.M.C.A., HILDEN, where they will be met by pipers and marched to their billets, the strictest attention being paid to march discipline.

   DRESS: Full Marching Order.

   Os. C. Coys. will ensure that there are no extra articles, such as mugs, etc. hanging on to the haversack or pack. Particular attention to be paid to this point.

3. Transport Officer will arrange transport this morning for officers' valises and any extra Coys Stores.

4. Relief complete will be wired to Orderly Room by each Coy. immediately after relief.

5. STORES.   A careful list of permanent stores handed over will be made and receipts obtained in duplicate, one copy being forwarded to Orderly Room on arrival of Coys. at HILDEN.

6. Os. C. Coys. will ensure that all billets, wash houses, etc. are left scrupulously clean, and a certificate will be obtained from an officer of the relieving party that this has been done. This certificate will be forwarded to Orderly Room on arrival of Coys. at HILDEN.

7. One Officer from "W", "X", and "Y" Coys. will remain on duty for 24 hours with the relieving unit at the Posts.

8. ACKNOWLEDGE.

Copy No. 1.   C.O.
  "   "   2.   "W" Coy.
  "   "   3.   "X" "
  "   "   4.   "Y" "
  "   "   5.   Q.M.
  "   "   6.   SIG. Off.
  "   "   7.   T.O.
  "   "   8.   R.S.M.
  "   "   9.   FILE.
  "   "   10. DIARY.
  "   "   11. Spare.

Issued at 11.00 by runner.

Capt. & Adjt.,
1/8 Scottish Rifles.

1/5th. Scottish Rifles.   SECRET.
OPERATION ORDER NO. 2.   Appendix III   COPY NO. 18

                                                23/6/19

REF. MAPS.
GERMANY 1., N.E. } 1/25,000
    "   2R, N.E. }

1. INFORMATION.

The 3rd. Lowland Bde. will advance to-morrow the 24th. inst. into unoccupied territory, commencing the march from the Starting Point, Road Junction, KLEEF, K43.68.
Sheet 2R, S.E. at Zero hour.
ZERO HOUR is 03.15.

2. INTENTION.

This Battalion will march to GRUITEN and occupy that village.
ROUTE: KLEEF, THILLS, MYLLRATH, GRUITEN STATION, GRUITEN.
If necessary the Battalion will come into action to obtain this objective.

3. INSTRUCTIONS.

The Battn. will parade in Column of Route in the HOCHDAHLER STRASSE, HILDEN, with the head of the Column resting on the MUHLEN STRASSE at ZERO - 30 minutes, in the following order:-
Hqrs., "W", "X", "Y", "Z" Coy. L.G. limbers will march in rear of their Coys.
1 Section D Coy. M.G.C. will march in rear of the Battn.

DRESS:- Fighting Order. The steel helmets will be slung on the left shoulder strap.

4. TRANSPORT.

The Transport will move under orders of the Transport Officer, as per instructions issued to him separately to-day.

5. RESISTANCE.

During the advance Red Verey Lights 1" will be fired by the Coys. concerned as a signal to indicate that their advance is being resisted by the enemy, and a detailed report on the situation will be sent, immediately to Btn. Hqrs.

6. CONTACT AEROPLANE.

Contact aeroplanes will fly a Yellow and Red Streamer from their tails, and will also carry black flaps attached to the rear edge of the lower plane, one on each side of the body. Ground sheets will be displayed at Btn. Hqrs. on arrival at GRUITEN, and kept out until further orders.

7. BLANKETS & PACKS.

All blankets will be rolled in bundles of 10, and with the men's packs, be stacked at Coy. Hqrs. at 01.30 hours.
Hqrs. Details blankets and packs will be stacked at Q.M. Stores at the same hour.
All officers' kits will be stacked ready for loading in baggage wagon at Q.M. Stores at 01.30.
T. O. will arrange for transport to report at this hour.
O. C. "W" Coy. will detail a loading party for these kits of 1 N.C.O. and 2 men.

8. BILLETING PARTY.

1 Man per Coy. and 1 man from Btn. Hqrs. will report with a bicycle to Capt. Dalrymple, M.C., at 02.00 hours to act as Billeting

(2).

1/8th. Scottish Rifles. OPERATION ORDER NO. 2. contd.

Party. This party will proceed with the Advance Guard under Major McEwen, M.C., 1/4th. R.S.Fs. Sig. Officer will arrange to issue 1 cycle to each Coy by 01.30 hours.

8. **GUARD.**

On arrival at GRUITEN STATION, "B" Coy. will remain there as guard. Instructions have been issued to O.C. "B" Coy. separately.

10. **STRAGGLERS.**

Each Coy. Cmdr. will detail one N.C.O. to march in rear of the Btn. to collect stragglers. 2/Lt. Renwick will be in charge of this party.

11. **GENERAL.**

(A). Major F. Eaves, D.S.O., will be in command of the Battn. whilst on the march. All reports will be sent to him at the head of the Btn.

(B). Coy. meat rations, vegetables, etc. will be carried on the Coy. Field Kitchens.

(C). Btn. Hqrs. will be established in GRUITEN. Until further instructions are issued, all reports will be sent to the Post Office there, where Hqrs. will be temporarily established.

(D). All previous Administrative Instructions issued hold good.

12. **ACKNOWLEDGE.**

```
COPY NO.   1  to  Cmdg. Officer.
   "    "   2   "  2nd. in Cmd.
   "    "   3   "  Adjutant.
   "    "   4   "  O.C. "B" Coy.
   "    "   5   "   "    "  "   "
   "    "   6   "   "    "  "   "
   "    "   7   "   "    "  "   "
   "    "   8   "  T.O.
   "    "   9   "  Q.M.
   "    "  10   "  S.O.
   "    "  11   "  M.O.,
   "    "  12   "  Lt. Burke, M.G.C.
   "    "  13   "  R.S.M.
   "    "  14   "  3rd. Low. Bde.
   "    "  15   "  1/4th. R.S.F.
   "    "  16   "  FILE.
   "    "  17   "  DIARY.
   "    "  18   "  SPARE.
```

Issued at 20.00 hours.

[signature]
Capt. & Adjt.,
1/8 Scottish Rifles.

SECRET. 1/8th. Scottish Rifles.   Appendix IV

OPERATION ORDER NO. 3.   COPY No. 12.

REF. MAPS.
DUSSELDORF.
SHEET 4. 1/25,000.   29th. June, 1919.

1. **INFORMATION.**
   The 1/8th. Scottish Rifles will tomorrow take over from the 8th. Royal Highlanders (Black Watch) the original Perimeter Posts and Guards held by the battalion before the present concentration at HILDEN.

2. **INTENTION.**
   "W" Coy. will relieve the Coy. 8th. Black Watch, at HIMMELGEIST;
   "X" Coy. will relieve the Coy. Black Watch at HOLTHAUSEN Barrier; and
   "Z" Coy. will relieve the Coy. 8th. Black Watch at RHENANIA Petrol Factory.

3. **INSTRUCTIONS.**
   (a) All Coy. baggage will be conveyed by Transport and will be stacked outside Coy. H.Q. by 12.00 hours to-morrow. Blankets will be rolled in bundles of 10, securely tied and labelled. Officers' kits will be ready for loading at Coy. H.Q. at 12.00 hours. Coy. L.G. Limbers will be packed under Coy. L.G. N.C.O. and will move off with Transport.
   Orders re. transport of palliasses will be issued later.
   (b) "W" Coy. and the right half of "X" Coy. will parade at the Church, HILDEN, at 13.30 hours, and "Z" Coy. and the left half of "X" Coy. at 14.00 hours ready to en-tram. O's. C. "W" and "Z" Coys. will arrange their own places to de-tram.
   (c) Dress. F.M.O. Steel Helmets will be on pack under supporting straps. Box Respirators will be slung.

4. **RATIONS.**
   Rations for 1st. July will be drawn to-morrow as usual at 12.00 hours, and will be carried up with Coy. baggage.

5. **TRANSPORT.**
   The T.O. will detail one G.S. Waggon each to report to O.C. "W" and "X" Coys. and 3 Limbers to report to O.C. "Z" Coy. at 12.00 hours. A second trip will be made if necessary to convey baggage.
   The T.O. will arrange for the delivery of Officers' chargers at the new positions, and that Field Kitchens report to "W", "X", "Z" Coys' cooks for any food stuffs before moving off.

6. **REQUISITIONED MATERIAL.**
   Coys. will take over all stores and requisitioned material previously handed over by them to the Black Watch. Duplicate receipts will be forwarded to Bn. H.Q.

7. **BILLETS.**
   O's. C. Coys. will ensure that all billets, wash-houses, latrines, etc. are left scrupulously clean, and will forward to Bn. H.Q. a certificate to this effect obtained from an officer of the Coy. relieved.

8. **RELIEF.**
   Relief will be completed by 18.00 hours. "Relief complete" will be wired to Bn. H.Q. at once.

9. **ACKNOWLEDGE.**   Issued at 20.20 hours
                                             by runner.

Copy No.	1.	C.O.
" "	2.	2nd..i/c.
" "	3.	Adj.
" "	4.	O.C. "W" Coy.
" "	5.	" "X" "
" "	6.	" "Y" " (for information)
" "	7.	" "Z" "
" "	8.	" H.Q. " (for information)
" "	b9.	T.O.
" "	10.	Q.M.
" "	11.	R.S.M. (for information)
" "	12.	Diary.
" "	13.	File.

No. 14 M.O. (for information)
"   15. 3rd. Low. Inf. Bde. (for information)
"   16. 8th. Black Watch. (for information).

George McNairy
Capt. a/adj.

for Lt. Col.,
Cmdg. 1/8th. Scottish Rifles.

Army Form C. 2118.

1/8 Bn SCOTTISH RIFLES

WAR DIARY
or
INTELLIGENCE SUMMARY.
(Erase heading not required.)

Place	Date 1919	Hour	Summary of Events and Information	Remarks and references to Appendices
HILDEN GERMANY	JULY 1ST		"W", "X", and "Z" coys on perimeter control posts. "Y" coy engaged on guards and interior economy. A Peace Drumhead Service was held at Battalion H.Q. Mess in the evening which was most enjoyable. Brig. Gen. E.S. Girdwood, C.B, C.M.G., with H.Q. all staff and Col. Mackenzie (G.S.L.I.) and other officers attended. The arrangements were admirably carried out by Lieut. Young.	
	2nd		Duties and Routine as for 1st inst.	
	3rd		Do.	
	4th		This day was observed as a holiday for all troops of the II Corps. In the evening a very successful Whist Drive and Open Air Concert was held in the Beer Garden, HILDEN, under Battalion arrangement, open to all troops in the neighbourhood. Brigade Major (Major Bowen) and Major Brown (G.S.L.3) G.H.Q. attended and assisted at the concert. The arrangements were most efficiently carried out by 2/Lt. Telfer, assisted by 2/Lt. Lamb. A proportion of officers and men from the control posts were given permission to attend.	
	5th		Duties and Routine as for 1st inst.	
	6th		Do. Divine Services, Presbyterian, C of E and R.C, in the nature of Peace Celebrations were held.	

(2) Army Form C. 2118.

WAR DIARY
or
INTELLIGENCE SUMMARY.
(Erase heading not required.)

1/8 Bn. SCOTTISH RIFLES

Place	Date 1919	Hour	Summary of Events and Information	Remarks and references to Appendices
HILDEN GERMANY	JULY 7th		Duties and Routine as for 1st. "Y" Coy. at disposal of Coy. Commander for interior economy. Lieut. H. & V. Barr, M.C., C. de G., No. V18939 C.Q.M.S. A. Partington M.M., C. de G., "Z" Coy. No. 290834 Sergt. C. Ramage, D.C.M., M.M., "W" Coy. No. 39263 Pte. J. Ironside, M.M. (H.Q. Coy.) No. 353038 Pte. O. Walker, M.M. (H.Q. Coy.) were chosen to represent the Battalion in the Allied Victory March in PARIS on 14th inst.	
	8th	9 a.m.	At 9 a.m. the Battalion entrained at HILDEN Station and proceeded to its new Billeting Area at KONIGSHOVEN where it arrived at 5 p.m. some of the transport proceeding by road.	
KONIGSHOVEN	9th		Routine as usual. Coys were at disposal of Coy Cmdrs for the purpose of re-arranging accommodation and generally settling down.	
	10th		Routine as usual. Coys still at disposal of Coy Cmdrs. The S.O. inspected billets during the morning.	
	11th		Coys still at disposal of Coy Cmdrs for interior economy.	
	12th		Coys remain at disposal of Coy Cmdrs for interior economy.	
	13th		Church Parades. C. of E. at 09.15 hours. Presbyterian at 10.00 hours on Bn. Parade Ground, R.C. at 08.30 hours in KONIGSHOVEN Parish Church.	
	14th		Coys were trained under Coy. arrangements to-day. Programme included Musketry and close Order Drill, Lewis Gun training and signalling. All the N.C.O's were lectured by the R.S.M. on the duties between	

(3) Army Form C. 2118.

1/8 BN. SCOTTISH RIFLES

WAR DIARY
INTELLIGENCE SUMMARY.
(Erase heading not required.)

Instructions regarding War Diaries and Intelligence Summaries are contained in F.S. Regs., Part II. and the Staff Manual respectively. Title pages will be prepared in manuscript.

Place	Date 1919	Hour	Summary of Events and Information	Remarks and references to Appendices
KONIGSHOVEN GERMANY	JULY 14th		ranks and the private rifle exercises "Esprit de Corps" and close order drill. In the afternoon the C.O., 5 other officers, 25 N.C.Os. and 50 other ranks attended a sports meeting given by the 159th Regt. d'Infanterie (Chasseurs d'Alpine) at OTZENRATH. After the sports the party were entertained to dinner and a most excellent concert in the evening. The C.O. fixed prices to be charged by civilians for washing the men's underclothing with the Burgomaster.	
	15th		The Battalion paraded on Bn. Parade Ground at 0930 hours, and after inspection by the Commanding Officer, proceeded on a Route March MORKEN- FRIMERSDORF- EPPRATH- HARFF- KONIGSHOVEN.	
	16th		"W" and "X" Coys fired musketry practice on the Brigade Range at MORKEN. "Y" and "Z" Coys were under Coy & Pl. ndrs. on their respective training grounds, and were exercised in close order drill and musketry, and the R.S.M. lectured all the N.C.Os. on various subjects. Several N.C.Os. and men proceeded on 4 days special leave to the British Empire Leave Club, COLOGNE. This leave has been going on for some time now, and is much appreciated by the men. Leave to U.K. for Other Ranks is on a generous scale, some 50 - O.Rs. proceeding per week, after being 4 months since last leave.	
	17th		As the boys were very much reduced in numbers, the whole Battalion proceeded to the Brigade Range at MORKEN and were exercised in musketry under Capt. J. B? Stewart. 2 Platoons from "Y" and "Z" Coys proceeded to HARFF to protect the Divisional stores from interference by civilians, who had broken into and looted stores the previous night.	

(4) Army Form C. 2118.

1/8 BN. SCOTTISH RIFLES.

WAR DIARY
or
INTELLIGENCE SUMMARY.
(Erase heading not required.)

Place	Date 1919	Hour	Summary of Events and Information	Remarks and references to Appendices
KONIGSHOVEN GERMANY.	JULY 18th.		"Y" and "Z" Coys. on MORKEN Range. "W" and "X" Coys. under Coy. arrangements were exercised in Coy. Drill, Musketry, and other subjects. Lieuts. F.J. Deacon, J.H. Manson, A. Macdonald and 2/Lt. S.R. McCall joined the Battalion for duty from U.K. and were posted to "W", "Y", "Z" and "Y" Coys. respectively.	
	19th.		Routine as usual. Coys. were medically inspected by the M.O during the morning, and as the day was ordered by Parliament to be a General Holiday, there were no further parades.	
	20th.		Church Parades: Presbyterian at 10.00 hours on Bn. Parade Ground. R.C. in KONIGSHOVEN R.C. Church at 08.30 hours. Lieuts. F.J. Deacon, J.H. Manson and A. Macdonald proceeded to join the 9th Battn. Scottish Rifles, and were struck off the Battalion strength accordingly. Capt. & R. Sattonstall M.C. having joined 3d. Lowland Inf. Bde. staff, was struck off the strength of the Battalion, as from 26/6/19. C. of E. Holy Communion at 08.00 hours and Voluntary evening service at 19.30 hours were held in the Recreation Room (above Divl. Canteen) HARFF.	
	21st.		"W" and "X" Coys. fired practices on the 30 yds. Range at KONIGSHOVEN "Y" and "Z" Coys. were engaged on Musketry Instruction, Coy. Drill and Box Respirator Drill and Inspection by Divl. Gas Officer.	
	22nd.		Coys. carried out training under Coy. Cmdrs. A Knock-out Football Competition between Coys., H.Q., and Transport to	

Army Form C. 2118.

(5)

WAR DIARY
or
INTELLIGENCE SUMMARY.
(Erase heading not required.)

1/8 Bn. SCOTTISH RIFLES

Place	Date 1919	Hour	Summary of Events and Information	Remarks and references to Appendices
KONIGSHOVEN GERMANY	JULY 22nd		To decide which team should play a match against the 159th Regt. d'Infanterie (Chasseur d'Alpin) on Saturday next, is in progress. The Battalion Wet Canteen is now open daily from 14.00 to 21.00 hours, and in full swing.	
	23rd		"Y" and "Z" Coys. received Educational Training in "Y" Coy. Dining Hall, and "W" "X" " " " "W" " Marquee from 09.15 to 11.15 hours. The instruction was given by the Brigade Educational N.C.Os. Sergts. Howard and Bell. From 11.15 to 12.30 the Q. Quartermaster inspected all Coy. Stores. Lieut (a/Capt.) J. Menary, M.C., 10th Bn., attached 1/8 Bn. Scottish Rifles, is appointed Adjutant of the Battalion, with effect from 27/6/19 vice Lieut. (T/Capt.) E.R. Saltmarshe, M.C., 5th Bn. Yorks. Regt., attached 1/8 Bn. Scottish Rifles, appointed Staff Captain, 3rd Lowland Inf. Bde. on 27/6/19. The one man per Coy. detailed to deal with the fly nuisance, known as the "Fly man", will in future be designated "Hygiene Man".	
	24th		The Cmdg. Officer, Lt.-Col. M. Findlay, D.S.O. has had the Territorial Decoration conferred upon him by H.M. the King. The 1/8 Bn. Scottish Rifles Guard was selected to represent the Bde. in the Life Guards which was inspected by Maj.-Gen. Judor, C.B., C.M.G. Corps. Comdr. Genl., who expressed himself as extremely pleased with our display. The Divl. Comdr. also Gen. E.S. Girdwood, C.B., C.M.G. has, however, had the R.S.C. (Chg) addressed a special letter of congratulation to the C.O. Complimenting the 4/T.O. (Lieut. T. Young) & his transport personnel.	

WAR DIARY
INTELLIGENCE SUMMARY

Army Form C. 2118.

Place	Date	Hour	Summary of Events and Information	Remarks and references to Appendices
KONIGSHOVEN GERMANY	25th (cont)		HQ Coy were defeated by "Z" Coy in the afternoon. A best match is played in the eliminating competition to decide the team to play for Brigade team at the Corps Inter-Allies sports. Farewell complimentary letter from Lieut. Col. Jacobs's letter of farewell. Division is quitting the Corps and Division weighs on an end. The men are busy preparing the sports round for the following day. Capt. Stewart & 2/Lt. Edge proceeded on course.	(A)
	26th		a.m. A football Match with the French Regiment from the neighbouring village of OTZENRATH, a most enjoyable day was spent. (See attached Account of Sports.) A lecture was given by an official lecturer in the forenoon. "The Great Air Ship" — by an official lecturer — the Scotch thistle on a blue ground — has been issued to the Battn a few men are wearing it for the first time.	(C)
	27th		The C.O. (Lt-Col. W.H. Findlay D.S.O.) proceeded on leave. Major J. Cavendish took over command of the Bn. the Lewises L.C. in C (Brevet W. Robertson) of the Rhine Army will visit the Bde area to-morrow the 29th inst. Lectures are to be undertaken.	(D)
	28th		We have drawn lots for our 18th - our Mr. Fray Betts Rifles up of the troops are 2 two march for a bath.	(E)

Army Form C. 2118.

1/8 Scottish Rifles

WAR DIARY
or
INTELLIGENCE SUMMARY
(Erase heading not required.)

Instructions regarding War Diaries and Intelligence Summaries are contained in F. S. Regs., Part II. and the Staff Manual respectively. Title pages will be prepared in manuscript.

Place	Date	Hour	Summary of Events and Information	Remarks and references to Appendices
KÖNIGSHOVEN. GERMANY.	29th		The Silver War Medal Ribbons have to-day been issued to the Battalion. The day has been spent in the improvement of Billets & Coys. are busy preparing for the new Pay & Mess Book System of accounts which begins on 1st August.	(A)
	30th		The usual training parades were carried out, to include Musketry, Lewis Range, Education & Coy Drill. The Officers went almost en masse to the Sports of the 1/4 R.S.F. at BEDBURG.	(A)
	31st		The C.O. (Major Lewis S2O) attended a meeting at Bde. H.Q. to arrange for a Bde. Rifle Meeting to be held about 21st August. For the following day: The idea of a Bde Gymkhana is being put forward to our Regt. Monted Paper Chase & all the Officers are looking forward to morrow.	(A)

Total Number demobilised during July 1919 1 officer, 13 O.Rs.
Effective Strength of the Bn at 31/7/19 — 29 Offs. 610 O.Rs.
Ration Strength " " " " — 19 " 308 O.Rs.

George R. Murray
Capt & Adjutant,
1/8 Sco. Rifles

31st July, 1919.

INTER-ALLIED SPORTS MEETING.
159e REG. d'INFANTERIE-ALPINE -- 1/8th. SCOTTISH RIFLES.

This Meeting took place at KONIGSHOVEN before a large gathering including Major-General Tudor, C.B. C.M.G. Cmdg. Lowland Division, Brig.-General Girdwood, C.B. C.M.G. Col. Brunet, Cmdg. 159e Reg. d' Infanterie-Alpine and nearly 200 Officers and men of this Regiment.

The sport was good, especially noteworthy being the excellent running and jumping of the Frenchmen. They made the high and long jumps their own, also the 100 and 200 yards flat races.

The 1500 Metres however, for which a cup was awarded, was won in fine style by Pte. Ferguson of the Royal Scots. In the Tug-of-War the Scottish Rifles were too strong for the visitors: this event was won by the 8th. Bn. Scottish Rifles Transport Team, who after a severe struggle, beat the R.S.F. Team after an extra pull.

A very interesting event was the Musical Chairs for Mounted Officers. The horses cantered to music rendered by the band of the 159th. Regt. d'Infanterie Alpine, which along with the pipers of the 1/4th. Bn. Scots Fusiliers, added to the afternoon's enjoyment by excellent selections.

A football match between teams from the Regt. Inf. Alpine and the 8th. Scottish Rifles resulted in a win for the latter by 1 -0. The visitors showed a good knowledge of the game, their quickness and absence of hesitation giving a lesson to their more experienced opponents.

At the close of the afternoon's events, the prizes were distributed by Major-Gen. Tudor, R.Sgt. Major Martichon of the 159th. Regt. came up for prizes six times: this cheery little soldier proving himself easily to be Victor Ludorum.

Col. Findlay then thanked Gen.Tudor for distributing the prizes, and cheers for him and for Gen.Girdwood and Col. Brunet were heartily given.

In the evening an Inter-Allied Concert took place. The French visitors gave a very bright exhibition of catchy songs. Sgt. Major Searles of the 8th. Scottish Rifles in story, dance and tongue-twisting song, reaped his usual harvest of laughter.

At the close Col. Findlay, D.S.O. addressed the visitors in a short complimentary speech and all joined in singing Auld Lang Syne, The Marseilleise and God Save the King.

R E S U L T S.

100 Yards Race.

1. Martichon,   159e Reg. Inf. Alpine.
2. Garino,   do.
3. Amelon,   do.

220 Yards Race.

1. Filliat,   do.
2. Vaughan,   1/8th. Scottish Rifles.
3. Barker,   H. L. I.

440 Yards Race.

1. Hanlon,   11th. Royal Scots.
2. Martichon,   159e Reg. Inf. Alpine.
3. Revelle,   do.

1500 Metres Race.

1. Ferguson.   11th. Royal Scots.
2. Richardson,   H. L. I.
3. Clark,   H. L. I.

Long Jump.

1. Martichon,   159e Reg. Inf. Alpine.
2. Sammartin,   do.
3. Filliat,   do.

High Jump.

1. Sammartin,   do.
2. Martichon,   do.
3. Druelle,   do.

Sack Race.

1. Lloyd,   1/8th. Scottish Rifles.
2. Barrer,   159e   Reg.d'Inf. Alpine.
3. Mousgnet,   do.

Mules Scurry.

1. Celsar,   do.
2. Watson,   9th. Scottish Rifles.
3. Gormley,   1/8th. Scottish Rifles.

WEEKLY TRAINING PROGRAMME.

UNIT................1/8th. SCOTTISH RIFLES.

Date.	Subject.	Area.	Time.	Remarks.
1919. July 14th.	Coy. Training.-L.Gunners under Coy. arrangements. Musketry.-(espy.Rapid loading, aiming & Rapid firing. All N.C.O's. under R.S.M. Lecture by Officers to men on "The Rest."- P.T. & R.T.	Sigs. on Btn. Football Field, "Y" & "Z" on Btn.Recreation Grd. "W" & "X" " " " Parade	09.00-10.00 10.00-11.00 11.00-12.00	All Sigs. under Bn.Sig.Officer. N.S.M's. programme attached.
15th.	Bn. Route March.		09.00-13.00	Route:Refce.Map(1K.1/100,000). Bn.Parade Ground(near Transport) MORKEN-FRIMERSDORF-track past Rifle Range to road junct.1/8" N.of E.in EPPRATH-HARFT-KONIGS-HOVEN.
16th.	Right Half Battn.on Range. Left Half Battn. as for 14th.	do.	09.00-12.00	
17th.	Bn. Route March.		09.00-13.00	Route:Refce.map(1K.1/100,000). Bn. Parade Ground(near Transport) Westward along KONIGSHOVEN-RUMDT Road to road junction 3/4"N. of 1" of KASTOR-N.E. along track to GARZWEILER-KONIGSHOVEN Road,by which to KONIGSHOVEN
18th.	Right Half Battn. as for 14th. Left Half Battn. on Range.	do.	09.00-12.00	
19th.	Kit Inspection by O.C. & 2nd.i/Command.		09.00-12.00	

ADDITIONAL REMARKS. Recreational Training each day 14.00 to 16.00 hours.
EDUCATION will be carried on in the following subjects:-
Gardening, Painting, Whitewashing, Roadmaking, Carpentry.

Capt. & A/Adjt.,
1/8th. Scottish Rifles.

2nd/our
8th S. Rifles

Army Form C. 2118.

WAR DIARY
or
INTELLIGENCE SUMMARY.
(Erase heading not required.)

Instructions regarding War Diaries and Intelligence Summaries are contained in F.S. Regs., Part II. and the Staff Manual respectively. Title pages will be prepared in manuscript.

Place	Date	Hour	Summary of Events and Information	Remarks and references to Appendices
KÖNIGSHOVEN	1/8/19		All the Coys were engaged on training or resting, special attention to musketry. The Officers of the Battalion were a Shooter Paper Chase which was attended by several Officers of Bde. Hqrs and the 9th Scottish Rifles. The Meet was at HARFF at 14.30 hours. A meeting was held to discuss up a programme for a Bde. Rifle meeting to be held at an early date. 3 Officers and 30 O.R.s proceeded to NIDEGGEN under Capt. Dalrymple to take part in the Cafe (?) outright testing.	(Bn.) to take (f-n)
	2/8/19		Lt Lovel Hqrs Coy had W. Coy. 1 – 0, after three spells of extra time. Arrangements were made with the French Troops at OTZENRATH and Col. RAT. to take part in our Rifle meeting.	(Bn.)
	3rd		The Rev Hazlett B.A delivered a lecture on V.D. One of Nones Zena Ashwell's Concert Parties visited BEDBURG and a party attended from the Battalion. There was a holiday and the Battalion team played the team of the French 159e Regt. d' Infanterie by 4 – 0.	(Bn.)
	4th			(Bn.)
	"			(Bn.)
	5th		At WEVELINGHOVEN the Lunch troops held at Steeple Chase over a very trying course. All the Officers of the Battalion went over to see the show. A Sports Officer, the M.G.C. was there in a big field. Col. Burnet wrote to make further arrangements about the Rifle Meeting.	(Bn.)
	6th		The Army Council are expected at HARFF nearly and we are to supply a Guard of Honour. This went in circulation to receive honours orders to prepare four Rotten boys and half of Hqrs Coy. with a total of 5 Officers only to HERBESTHAL.	(Bn.) gazette 4/3/--
	7th		At 06.00 hours the Detachment for HERBESTHAL moves off entraining at BEDBURG	APPENDIX OPERATION ORDER No 4

(A8001) D. D. & L., London, E.C. Wt. W17771/M2091 750,000 5/17 Sch. 82 Forms/C2../6/14

Army Form C. 2118.

WAR DIARY
or
INTELLIGENCE SUMMARY.
(Erase heading not required.)

Instructions regarding War Diaries and Intelligence Summaries are contained in F. S. Regs., Part II. and the Staff Manual respectively. Title pages will be prepared in manuscript.

Place	Date	Hour	Summary of Events and Information	Remarks and references to Appendices
KONIGSHOVEN.	8th.		Only a very few men of the Battalion remain at KONIGSHOVEN and these are engaged clearing up and collecting arms stores. Arms stores are still being collected.	
	9th.			
	10th.		C.O. and a number of the Officers drove down to the French 1st. on 3rd. Battn. R.I.A. to say "Au revoir" in case we should move soon.	
	11th.		The Battn. team beat the 1st Battn. team of the 159e. R.I.A. by 4 goals to 1 at GUSTORF. We are in very close liaison with the French – the team was entertained by the French troops and 6 of our Officers were the guests of Major Trombley at dinner. The Major has a great liking for things British.	
	12th.		Early morning parade at 07.00 hrs. as intended our move. The C.O. and dept. and Staff/dept. reconnoitred a course for a Cross Country Paper Chase. Arrangements.	
	13th.		Our Paper Chase took place at 17.00 hours with Capt. Nicholl and Lieut. Rogers A.F. as drawer. 3 French Officers took part.	
	14th.		The French 1st. Battn. of the 159e. R.I.A. passed through KONIGSHOVEN on a route march and impressed us by their turn-out. They were to bivouac the building party of the 51st. Batt. ("B" Battery) arrived to take over part of the village.	
	15th.		20 men attended the Torchlight Tattoo at NIDEGGEN, when 30 of our men and 3 Officers are taking part in the chorus. Mons. Lina Schunelli County Party produce "Mon Coerage Necklace".	

WAR DIARY or INTELLIGENCE SUMMARY

Army Form C. 2118.

Place	Date	Hour	Summary of Events and Information	Remarks and references to Appendices
KÖNIGSHOVEN	16th		C.O. and several Officers went to see the Spotlight Tattoo at NIDEGGEN. A warning order is received by the Battalion that it will proceed to U.K. on 25th inst.	(A)
	17th		Owing to the scattered billets, men are all gathered into a rest camp of marquees and bell-tents. Another Paper Chase is held by the Battn. which is attended by Brig. Gen. Girdwood, several of the Bde. Staff, Officers from the 9th Scottish Rifles and 4 1/4 R.S.F. and about 20 men of the Transport were on mules. We have a sports afternoon.	(B)
	18th.		A Board of Officers audited the stores and messes in the Q.M's department. With the gradual daily return of men from leave Battn. at KÖNIGSHOVEN is becoming much stronger. Incoming parades are re-commenced and the R.S.M. takes all Battalion for the handling of arms. Education is resumed. Spotlight Tattoo Party returns from NIDEGGEN.	(C)
	19th		All personnel at KÖNIGSHOVEN were engaged in ordinary training e.g. drill & handling of arms, and also in education.	
	20th.		Company drill forms the main part of the training, with the remainder of the morning spent in cleaning up for movement move. The 9th Batt. hold its sports at NEURATH and a number of the Officers attended these for the afternoon. Col. A.J. Macher, C.M.G, formerly 2nd Batt. and 10th Battn. now there from COLOGNE. The Battn. played the "B" 51st Bde. R.F.A. at soccer and lost by 3-0. A Bde. Mounted Paper Chase took place at BEDBURG at 18.00 hrs. There was a large field and the meeting however highly enjoyable.	(D) (E)
	21st.			

Army Form C. 2118.

WAR DIARY
or
INTELLIGENCE SUMMARY.
(Erase heading not required.)

Instructions regarding War Diaries and Intelligence Summaries are contained in F. S. Regs., Part II. and the Staff Manual respectively. Title pages will be prepared in manuscript.

Place	Date	Hour	Summary of Events and Information	Remarks and references to Appendices
KONIGSHOVEN	22nd		Administration Instructions No 5 (to accompany Operation Order No 6) was issued to all concerned. Coys spent the day on internal economy.	
	23rd		The Companies made employed cleaning up for the Coy Officers FMO inspection to take place on the 25th inst.	
	24th		There were no Church Parades.	
	25th		The Battalion was inspected, by Coys, by the Commanding Officer during the forenoon. The dress was FMO and the object was to ensure uniformity in Coys by pointing out variations in turn-out. 16 Men were demobilized under AO 55, recommended by AO 292. This is the first batch of the Destiny men. Men who had been employed on the 25th were inspected by the Commanding Officers. Every man in the Battalion has been inspected in FMO.	
	26th		B/51 RFA held a mounted paper chase attended by whole Staff & Officers of the 8th & 9th. The shout was at KONIGSHOVEN at 11,00 hrs and the course was 9 miles long. Despite the drenching rain the meeting was very successful.	
	27th		Coys spent part of the morning cleaning after out SAA.	
	28th		Battalion paraded in Mass – Inspection in FD drill movements. The Commanding Officer addressed in full respects to the Battn. on the good conduct to the march in putting the men.	

D. D. & L., London, E.C.
Wt. W2771/M2031 750/C00 5/17 Sch. 52 Forms C2118/14

WAR DIARY
or
INTELLIGENCE SUMMARY.
(Erase heading not required.)

Army Form C. 2118.

Place	Date	Hour	Summary of Events and Information	Remarks and references to Appendices
Krinkhorn	29th		Bns were at low disposal of Coy Cdrs. for packing and clearing up the Camp.	(A)
	30th		Officers inspection parade (less a hospital men etc) in F.M.D at 11.15 hours. Packing was completed for the move of equipment and stores, tomorrow. A cross country run took place and 16 entrants. The course was about 3 miles. "X" Coy won with "Z" Coy second. A very light display took place at 21.30 hrs.	(B)
	31st		The equipment known left HARFF at 13.51 taking vehicles and most of our stores. 2/Lt. McLeo was in charge of the equipment guard. Battalion paraded in Square at 10.30 hrs to review by Brig Genl Crozier, Cdn. 9th Inf Bde" to the Battalion reminding them of its work in the past and exhorting them to uphold its good name in the future.	
			Total numbers embarking during August 1919 Officers - O.R. 22 - 556	
			Battn. Strength of the Bn at August 31st 1919 Officers 30 - 23 - 511	
			Return " " " " " " "	
			Capt & Adjt. 1/9th Battn. R. Rifles	
			31 8/19.	

SECRET. 1/8th. Scottish Rifles.

OPERATION ORDER NO. 4.   Copy No...... 12

Reference Map 1L
1/100,000.   6th. August, 1919.

1. **INFORMATION AND INTENTION.**
    The Battalion (less Transport and members of H.Q. Coy. to be detailed by O.C. H.Q. Coy.) will move to HENRESTAL tomorrow, to take over Frontier Posts from Highland Division.

2. **INSTRUCTIONS.**
    (1) "W" Coy. will proceed under command of 2/Lieut. Hutchison; "X" Coy. under 2/Lieut. McGowan; "Y" Coy. under 2/Lieut. Lamb; "Z" Coy. under Capt. Kennedy, and the personnel of H.Q. who are moving under Lieut. Young. Capt. Kennedy will be in command whole detachment and Lieut. Young will act as Adjutant and Q.M. to detachment. No other officers will proceed. Canteen and Library will remain here.
    (2) Baggage lorries will report to all Coys. H.Q. tonight to collect all Coy. stores to be taken to new area. Baggage will be packed tonight in lorries and also blankets rolled in bundles of 10, securely tied and labelled. Kits of Officers proceeding will be packed on lorries tonight, also Coy. Lewis Gun Limbers will be packed tonight and with cookers will be taken to the Transport field tomorrow at 06.00 hours. Straw of palliasses will be emptied in a central Coy. dump and palliasses will be packed and taken with Coys.
    (3) All personnel proceeding will parade at Batn. Orderly Room at 05.30 hours tomorrow, ready to embus.
    (4) **Dress.** Full Marching Order, Steel Helmets will be on pack under supporting straps. Box respirators will be slung.

3. **RATIONS AND DIXIES.**
    Rations for 8th. inst. will be drawn from Q.M. Stores tonight at an hour to be named by the Q.M. Dixies, and boilers of cookers (if required) will be taken.

4. **TRANSPORT.**
    L.G. Limbers (loaded) and Field Kitchens will be collected at 06.00 hours tomorrow and parked at Transport Field. Limbers have been detailed by T.O. to report to all Coys. tonight to move stores required to be stacked near Q.M. Stores.

5. **STORES.**
    (a) Crockery and tables and marquees will be handed over to Q.M.
    (b) Area stores will be conveyed by limbers to dumps to be made near Q.M. Stores. Loading and off loading parties will be supplied by Coys. concerned. Coys. will prepare list of stores so dumped. Rifle racks will be taken to new area, if sufficient accommodation can be found on lorries.
    (c) Pioneers material will be collected from workshop after departure of personnel moving.

6. **BILLETS.**
    All billets, wash-houses, latrines and Coy. areas will be left scrupulously clean. This will be reported to the Adjt., in writing, before moving off.

7. **ARRIVAL.**
    Arrival in new area will be reported to Battn. H.Q. by wire.

8. **ACKNOWLEDGE.**

                                        Issued by runner at 11.55 hours.

    Distribution.
    Copy No. 1 C.O.   Copy. No. 7 O.C. H.Q. Coy.
    "   "   2 Adjt.   "   "   8 T.O.
    "   "   3 O.C. "W" Coy.   "   "   9 Q.M.
    "   "   4 "   "X" "   "   " 10 R.S.M.
    "   "   5 "   "Y" "   "   " 11 Bde. H.Q.
    "   "   6 "   "Z" "   "   " 12 Diary
                                "   " 13 File
                                                (Signed) George Menary.
                                                    Capt. & Adjt.,
                                                    1/8th. Scottish Rifles.

File War Diary

SECRET. TRANSFER OF THE BATTALION TO THE U.K.

GENERAL ADMINISTRATIVE INSTRUCTIONS No. 5.

TO ACCOMPANY OPERATION ORDER No. 5.

24

Diary

1. **PERSONNEL TRAINS.**
   Personnel with arms, personal equipment, Lewis Guns complete, will move by rail, via BOULOGNE or CALAIS.
   Composition of trains: 47 covers, 1 coach, 2 brakes.
   Length of journey by rail: about 36 hours.

2. **EQUIPMENT TRAINS.**
   (i) Vehicles and regimental equipment will proceed by rail via ANTWERP and will be loaded at entraining station by the Battalion.
   Composition of trains: 35 flats, 1 coach, 3 covers.
   Length of journey by rail: about 14 hours.
   (ii) Baggage Supply waggons shewing War Establishment as attached to units will accompany the transport of units, and will not move with the Divisional train.
   (iii) No personal kit is to be put on equipment trains. Any kit of this nature on these trains will be taken off at the Base and will not be sent to ENGLAND.

3. **ANIMALS.**
   Animals will be sent via CALAIS under seperate instructions. As animals will probably preceed transport arrangements will be made to provide the necessary animals to move transport to entrainment station.
   Only 7 riders (Class T or E) will proceed to U.K. from this Battn. Care must be taken to ensure that the disposal of animals is recorded. A list will be forwarded to the Div. "Q" before leaving, giving disposal of "T" and "E" horses and "S" horses and all mules.

4. **ADVANCE PARTY.**
   An advance party will be sent to the first personnel train leaving the entraining station at HARFF.

5. **ENTRAINMENT AND DETRAINMENT OFFICER.**
   (a) A Staff Officer will entrain the Battn. personnel at each station.
   (b) A Staff Officer will entrain the Battn. equipment at each station.
   (c) A Staff Officer will detrain the Battn. personnel at each station.
   (d) Under instructions of the Base Commandant, ANTWERP, equipment trains will be detrained.
   (e) In addition to these Entrainment and Detrainment Staff Officers mentioned above, 2/Lieuts. Johannes & West will assist R.T.O. at each station concerned re personnel and equipment respectively.

6. **ENTRAINING STATION.**
   O's.C. "W", "X", "Y", "Z", HQ., T.O. Q.M. will before marching off from KONIGSHOVEN hand to the Adjutant an Entrainment statement shewing-
   (according as it applies to each)
   (i) No. of Officers and Other Ranks.
   (ii) No. of vehicles, 4 wheeled, limbered.
   (iii) " " " 4 wheeled, not limbered.
   (iv) " " " 2 wheeled.
   (v) Amount of baggage in tons, stores etc., other than in vehicles.
   All vehicles, packages etc. are to be clearly marked with the name of Battalion.
   All packages must be securely packed

7. **TIMES OF REPORTING TO R.T.O.**
   The Battalion will report to R.T.O. at entraining station (HARFF) as follows:-
   (1) For personnel train 1 hour) before schedules time of departure
   (2) For equipment train 3 hours) of the trains.

8. **LOADING AND UNLOADING PARTIES.**
   O's.C. "Y" and "Z" Coys. will each provide 40 men as loading and unloading parties respectively at each entraining and detraining station. (Parties at ANTWERP will be provided by the Base Commandant).

Continued.

GENERAL ADMINISTRATIVE INSTRUCTIONS NO. 5 Continued.   Page 2.

9. RAILWAY. MISCELLANEOUS.
   (i) Entrainment will be completed ½ hour before departure of train.
   (ii) No soldier will detrain until ordered by an Officer.
   (iii) All doors of trucks on the **right** hand side (**left** hand side in Germany) will be kept closed.
   (iv) Brake vans are entirely for use of Railway staff, neither personnel nor baggage may be loaded in them.
   (v) Carriages and station premises are to be left clean.
   (vi) The R.T.O. is in supreme control at his station, his decision on all matters relating to railway working or station precinct is final.

10. SUPPLIES.
    (i) All men will entrain with rations sufficient to last them up to and including day after entrainment.
    (ii) Each Officer and O.R. will carry the Iron Ration.
    (iii) The Q.M. will indent for the necessary Iron Rations which should be drawn on the 25th. inst.

11. HALTE REPAS.
    Halte Repas will be provided at HUY, CHARLEROI, GHISLENGHIEN and HERRIES.
    The probable times of halting at these places will be notified.
    NOTE. As French money only can be accepted at HALTE REPAS. Company Commanders will ensure that all men are paid out in French currency prior to entraining. Separate instructions have been issued to Coys. re Pay.

12. ORDNANCE.
    (i) The clothing as laid down in A.R.O. 2789 will be taken by the men together with the second suit issued under Second Army Routine Order 2435 of the 24/1/19. The question of transport of the second suit is under consideration. Meantime, however, Coys. should consider the best method to adopt. It is suggested that bales or packing cases might be used.
    (ii) Box Respirators will be carried on the person.
    (iii) Stores of value and easily portable, i.e. bicycles, binoculars, watches, compasses, telescopes and rifles with telescopic sights, will be handed in to Ordnance under arrangements to be notified by D.A.D.O.S.
    Typewriters and duplicators will accompany personnel to U.K. A return will be forwarded to D.D., A.P. & S.S. shewing make and registered number of all such machines.
    Lists will be made in duplicate of all stores so handed in and a receipt obtained by Battn. on one copy, the other copy being retained by the officer to whom the stores are handed over.
    (iv) All stores and equipment additional surplus to A.F.G. 1098 are to be handed to Ordnance under instructions to be issued by D.A.D.O.S. Lists of articles so handed in are to be rendered to the Ordnance Officer taking them over.
    No equipment in A.F.G. 1098 which, in the opinion of the C.O., is considered unserviceable, will be taken home.
    Unserviceable articles should only be replaced if required for immediate use. Mere deficiences in A.F.G. 1098 will NOT be made good.
    Certificate from C.O. that all surplus stores have been handed in will be rendered to D.A.D.O.S. together with a statement of any deficiencies under A.F.G. 1098.
    (v) All tentage will be handed in dry, to D.A.D.O.S. as soon as it becomes available, and in any case, prior the the departure of the Battn.
    (vi) One blanket will accompany each man. The other blanket being handed in under para. 12 (iv).

13. BATHS.
    (i) All men should be bathed and their clothing deloused before entraining.
    (ii) Each man is to entrain wearing a clean suit of underclothing, plus a second clean suit in his pack.

Continued.

GENERAL ADMINISTRATIVE INSTRUCTIONS No. 5 Continued.   Page 3

14. REGIMENTAL EQUIPMENT.

Vehicles, stores, and equipment for entrainment for ANTWERP will be collected as close to the railhead as possible, due consideration being given to the necessity of preserving articles from the wet. Transport will be parked at KARFF.

A guard of 2/Lieut. Kenwick and 4 men of "Y" Coy. will remain with this equipment and accompany it to ANTWERP. When this equipment is embarked, the goods will be despatched by the Base Commandant, ANTWERP, to rejoin the Battalion in U.K. This guard will be provided with sufficient pay in advance to last them for 5 or 6 days at least, while at the Base.

It is essential that the regimental equipment of each Coy. should be kept separate throughout.

A list of packages despatched by the Battalion will be forwarded (in triplicate) by Q.M. and O's.C. Coys. and Signals Officer to Battn. Orderly Room by 12.00 hours on day prior to departure from MONTGHOVEN. N.B.:- Private stores, any requisitioned articles or unauthorised vehicles, are are not to be sent with Battalion's equipment to ANTWERP. Any stores in excess of A.F.G. 1098 are liable to be confiscated.

15. REQUISITIONED STORES.

All requisitioned articles including furniture, pianos, mess equipment, etc., will be handed in to the Local Burgomaster concerned and a detailed receipt obtained by 2/Lieut. Telfer.

16. AMMUNITION.

Ammunition will be returned into Depots, less S.A.A. 60 rounds carried on the man and the equipment. S.A.A. for Lewis Guns which will go with these guns in the personnel trains. Limbers proceed with the Battalion's equipment. Bombs, Grenades will be de-detonated under 2/Lieut. Lamb in accordance with instructions issued separaretl to this Officer and the Q.M.

17. CANTEEN.

2/Lieut. Telfer will ensure that all Canteen and all other outstanding accounts of the Battalion are settled before the departure of the Battalion.

George Menary,
Capt. & Adjt.,
1/8th. Scottish Rifles.

Distribution.

No. 1 Copy	C.O.	No. 7 Copy	O.C. "Y" Coy.
" 2 "	Adjt.	" 8 "	" "Z" "
" 3 "	Q.M.	" 9 "	" HQ. "
" 4 "	T.O.	" 10 "	3rd. Low. Bde.
" 5 "	O.C. "W" Coy.	" 11 "	File.
" 6 "	" "X" "	" 12 "	Diary.

Army Form C. 2118.

1/8 Bn Scottish Rifles

WAR DIARY
or
INTELLIGENCE SUMMARY.
(Erase heading not required.)

Place	Date	Hour	Summary of Events and Information	Remarks and references to Appendices
GERMANY KONIGSHOVEN	1/9/19		The Battalion paraded at 10.00 hours in the Camp and moved off at 10.15 for HARFF, by march route, where it entrained for CALAIS, travelling by troop train. The whole of the Brigade and many of the Divisional Staff were present to see the Battalion off. By the kindness of Brig. Gen Girdwood, Comdg 3rd Low. Bde., the Battalion received an excellent train ration from Brigade Canteen as a gift. The whole day was spent in the train, and the Battalion halted at HUY (Halte Repas) where a meal was served under official army arrangements. The night was spent in the train.	
FRANCE	2/9/19		Reveille at 06.00 hours found the train halted at GHISLENGHIEN (Halte Repas). The journey took us through much of the old devastated area and through Lille. The Battalion had a meal at MERRIS (Halte Repas) at about 14.30 hours. ARMENTIERES and "No man's land" presented interesting sights en route. CALAIS was reached at 20.00 hours, and the Battalion was put up in No 5 Camp (Officers in No 8 Camp).	

(2)

Army Form C. 2118.

1/8 Bn Scottish Rifles

WAR DIARY
or
INTELLIGENCE SUMMARY.
(Erase heading not required.)

Instructions regarding War Diaries and Intelligence Summaries are contained in F. S. Regs., Part II. and the Staff Manual respectively. Title pages will be prepared in manuscript.

Place	Date	Hour	Summary of Events and Information	Remarks and references to Appendices
FRANCE	3/9/19		The Battalion entrained in "Maid of Orleans" at 12.00, and after a speedy crossing, arrived at DOVER after 13.00 hours, having finished its Overseas Service. The Battalion was now en route for Home Station at the Curragh, Ireland, after being on Active Service for 4 years 102 days.	(M)

George McNary
Capt. & Adjt.,
1/8 Scottish Rifles.

Rath Camp, Curragh, Ireland
12th September, 1919.

www.ingramcontent.com/pod-product-compliance
Lightning Source LLC
Chambersburg PA
CBHW081457160426
43193CB00013B/2517